Gardening The High Sierra

Rick & Karen Dustman

For those who came before us, who taught us. And for those who come after, who want to learn!

First Edition

Copyright 2019 - Rick & Karen Dustman
All Rights Reserved

Clairitage Press

Printed in the United States

Introduction

Rick has been sticking seeds in the soil since the age of five, when an aunt first placed a hoe in his hand. He was a natural, taking to gardening — well, like a seed to good soil.

Over the past 50 years, he's been putting that natural green thumb to good use by figuring out ways to make all his gardens thrive, while living at elevations over 5,000 feet.

Gardening here in the Sierra takes a bit of a trick. It means more than just finding the right short-season, cold-tolerant varieties to plant. It also means figuring out just when to start planting, how to protect your hard work from a wide array of varmints, and finding the best ways to put up your garden bounty.

Friends are always asking Rick for gardening advice. So we wanted to share Rick's hard-won gardening tips with our friends and family. And of course you can't have a garden book without a few favorite recipes at the end. So we added those, too.

We hope this little book helps *your* high mountain garden to thrive!

Greenhouses & the Garden Calendar

Greenhouses: A greenhouse is a must-have here, where the seasons are so short. Make do with a cheapie if you must; but consider it a long-term investment. A good greenhouse will pay you back, year after year, as you buy fewer expensive six-paks from the Big Box stores and grow more yourself from seed.

We love ours (a Riga). It's withstood a dozen tough years, now, with all our usual sun, rain and deep snow. Hail has pecked holes in the exterior polycarbonate panels, but it's still sturdy and watertight.

The Riga's initial installation was definitely not for the faint of heart, though. German-engineered, its pieces fit together like a precision piece of equipment (which it is, after all). And some of the instructions were even in German! Assembly required strict attention to detail and a fair amount of patience to get everything lined up just right.

Because winds here have reached 122 mph, we secured the structure with metal L-brackets to a concrete perimeter foundation (12" deep, 6" wide) to make sure our expensive greenhouse didn't wind up in someone else's yard.

Metal L-brackets are bolted to a 6-inch wide concrete foundation to hold the greenhouse down securely in heavy wind.

Whatever model you buy, make sure your greenhouse comes with a *pneumatic roof opener* to automatically air out the inside when it gets too hot. You don't want the summer sun to cook your tender seedlings.

If your winds are anything like ours, you'll also want to consider building a *windbreak* on the gusty side to protect your investment from the worst of the wind stress.

After much trial-and-error, here's what Rick came up with. It's assembled on a metal frame, welded together and anchored firmly in concrete. (It helps to be a welder!) Replaceable plastic trellis panels (or you could use wood) are secured to the frame with plastic mounting strips along the edges, using sheet-metal screws. The open panels won't shade your greenhouse, yet interrupt the wind flow just enough for a decent windbreak.

Plastic strips made of the same material as the lattice secure each edge to the frame. Right: Back side of the welded metal frame.

Expect to have to replace those plastic panels over time, as the wind eventually rattles them loose and breaks the plastic retaining strips. But replacing panels and retaining strips is no big deal; just loosen the screws and swap out the panels and strips, and you're good to go for another three or four years.

Planting Calendar: So, *when* do you start planting what? The answer, of course, is part art and part science, part guess-work and part simply keeping an eye on the unique "signs and conditions" of each year.

We've kept a gardening calendar for more than a dozen years. It helps us remember when Spring rolls around each year with that inevitable question, "So *when* did we plant the beans last year?" We also include notes about the general climate of each month, so we remember what to expect.

Every year will bring somewhat different conditions, of course. You'll notice that we often list ranges rather than exact dates in our list below, reflecting the differences we've experienced over the years in planting conditions. So use this as just a general guide, and adjust as needed for your own microclimate.

Now is a great time to start your own calendar. Be sure to makes notes about what *didn't* work out as well as what did. You'll be glad you have it when next year rolls around!

Our Garden Calendar:

Winter: (Dec/Jan/Feb)

- Dec. 10 - It's cold, grey, and we've usually had at least one good snow by now. But it's less than two weeks to the Solstice!
- Dec. 21 - Winter Solstice, the happiest day of the year around here! The days are finally getting longer again.
- End of January we often get a big snow. The willows have a red haze on the ends, though, offering hope Spring is ahead.
- February 1 "turns the corner on winter" here, although all of January and the first half of Feb. tend to be cloudy and grey.
- Feb. 3 - 17 - Time to prune fruit trees and grapevines, before the sap starts running.
- Feb. 15 - New little green leaves appear on the native bitterbrush, and new green leaves start to show up in the lawn. Aspen trees begin to put out fuzzy catkins and buds about this time.
- By late February the willows are red and tiny buds are visible on the ends of the trees. Days are noticeably longer, and you can feel Spring in the air. Time to transplant iris bulbs.

Spring: (Mar/Apr/May)

- Mar. 3 - Columbine plants will be coming up in the flower beds. Time to start looking for onion starts.
- Mar. 14 - 31 - Plant onions in the garden.
- Mar. 15 - 21 - The "week when everything

changes"! And that makes total sense, as March 21st is the Spring Equinox. Willows are orange and starting to come out; and trees have big, fat buds. Pansies can be planted any time between now and mid-May.

- Mar. 25 - First leaf appears on our aspen trees!
- Mar. 15 - 31 - Time to clean out flower beds. Lawns will be mostly green by now and ornamental willow trees will have a "green haze" at the top.
- Mar. 22 - 30 - Start flowers in the greenhouse: bachelor button, coreopsis; snapdragon; marigolds; Chinese forget-me-nots; bluebells; larkspur.
- Mar. 20 - April 20 - Keep an eye on the asparagus! You'll be able to harvest fresh shoots now.
- End of March - Expect lots of wind, even some snow flurries.
- April 1 - Lilacs will have nearly-open buds and the first green leaves will begin to appear on the aspens. The entire month of April tends to be cold, windy, rainy, cloudy, and it may even snow 2-3 times. In between those episodes, however, it will be sunnier (if still cold). Trees are starting to come out.
- April 1 - 15 - Plant tomatoes and peppers in the greenhouse.
- April 21 - 26 - The weather is *gorgeous*, but unpredictable! End-of-April snowstorms are still possible.
- May tends to run 40 to 70 degrees. Lawns will be green!

- May 7 - 14 - Leaves start appearing on the grapevines.
- May 25 - The "perfect flower week," when our columbine and other flowers are at their showy peak.
- May 31 - Count on the "Memorial Day Snow" sometime near the end of May.

Summer: (June/July/Aug)

- June 21 - Summer Solstice.
- July 8 - 23 - Time to begin saving columbine, lupine, and other flower seeds for next year.
- July 8 - Freeze basil and cilantro (in freezer baggies or as pesto).
- July 12 - Aug 15 - Pick currants.
- July 27 - Aug 18 - First tomatoes are ready for eating! And pick peaches!
- Aug. 6 - Trim dead blooms from columbine and giant lupine, leaving only the still-green leaves.
- Aug. 15 - Nights are getting cooler.
- Aug. 15 - 31 - Time to put up tomatoes. Save seeds from dried snow pea pods.

Fall: (Sept/Oct/Nov)

- Late Aug - Sept 10 - Pick grapes; finish up tomatoes. Apples will be looking tempting but it's still too early for Jonathan and Gala varieties.
- Sept 9 - Aspens are beginning to turn; the sun is *just* starting to come up at 6:30 a.m. Allergy season may be in full swing.
- Sept 21 - Fall Equinox.

- Sept 23 - It's getting cold enough to start a fire. Time to finish gathering the last of the seeds.
- Oct 1 - October is a beautiful month - crisp and clear and the aspens are vibrant with a shimmery, translucent gold. If there hasn't been a freeze yet, pick the last of the tomatoes!
- Oct 7 - Aspens are golden; the burning bush is brilliant red.
- Oct 15 - A cold snap or two has reduced pollen levels a bit.
- Oct 28 - The first snow. (Typically just a skiff.)
- Oct 30 - Daylight Savings Time. (Can't we ever get rid of this silly bit of masochism?!)
- Nov 9 - 20 - The first _good_ snow. The cold snap has finally put an end to the flowers.
- November is a "hibernation month," a great time to rest, make great soup from the garden-stocked larder, study gardening magazines, and think ahead to *next* year's garden!

Seeds, Sets & Supplies

What should you plant here? Start with what you like to eat, of course!

Here are some varieties Rick especially likes and we've found do well here:

Tomatoes:

Rick's favorite tomato variety is the Beefmaster (a variety of beefsteak tomato, perfect for sandwiches). He'll typically plant four rows of those, with roughly 40 plants. He also highly favors the San Marzano, a smaller Roma-type tomato that's great for soup and tomato sauce. Not quite as many of those go in, usually "just" two rows. All told, our garden has been known to include as many as 77 prolific tomato plants, spitting out enough juicy red sauce to nearly float a battleship!

There's no doubt about it, though; the high point of every gardening year is the mid-summer day when the first tomato is ready to eat!

Peppers:

Peppers of all kinds do well here. We plant red, green and orange bells; long, mild Anaheims; and a relatively new miniature variety charmingly called Lunchbox peppers, which are extremely sweet and perfect for sandwiches, snacking, and (yes!) lunchboxes.

Roma-type tomatoes (like these San Marzanos) are long and slender. Meatier than their round cousins, they are perfect for salads, soups and sauces.

Onions:

For years, Rick planted onions from *onion sets*, those miniature bulbs that come in plastic mesh bag. They did oh-kay. But a few years ago he switched from sets to thin, grass-like *onion starts*. And he's never looked back. Red, yellow, and white onions all do well here. Just pop the tiny plants straight into the ground once all danger of frost is over.

Cucumbers/Pickles:

Cucumbers are another staple crop around here. Once Rick found a recipe that duplicated Grandma Levoff's Dill Pickles, which he remembered from his childhood, pickle-making is a favorite summer activity. (We've included the recipe in the back of this book.)

Just remember when you buy seed: there *is* a difference between eating-cucumbers and pickling-cucumbers. The type meant for salads has a thinner skin and won't be quite as robust in size as the pickling variety.

Greens:

Head lettuce has just never done well at Rick's Garden. Leaf lettuces like romaine and mesclun have been edible, but the leaves tend to be tough (possibly from our snappy spring nights), and the plants bolt quickly.

We've had better luck with Spinach, and Bok Choi grows fabulously here.

Our current favorite green, though, is Miner's Lettuce — once a staple for early miners over in Gold Country. We plant it in a wooden barrel on the back porch so it gets plenty of sun in the mornings but afternoon shade. The barrel also helps contain what otherwise can be a freely-spreading plant. The tender leaves make a delightful alternative to regular lettuce!

Miner's Lettuce is a delightful micro-green. Our patch shares a wooden barrel with a blueberry bush.

Be forewarned: deer love it as much as we do. We cover the barrel with wire mesh during deer season.

Beans & Peas:

Snow peas (also known as Chinese peas) are a favorite early crop for us. You'll need to protect them from hungry mice until the plants are up several inches, or the critters will have a feast. Give the plants something to climb on, and stand back. When the tender pods are coming on, they're prolific!

For green beans, Rick likes the string-less Blue Lake variety. They're also great for canning.

Most other bean varieties do well for us, too. Among the ones we've grown are Jacob's Cattle Beans (a white bean with pretty magenta splotches); Navy beans, black beans, and fava beans. We're excited to try growing piquinto (small red) beans next year to use in a Santa Maria-style bean dish.

Herbs:

Basil, cilantro, dill, rosemary, sage, and thyme all thrive in our yard. Rick plants the basil along the edges of his garden. The dill gets its own garden row; and the smaller herbs like sage, rosemary, and thyme are confined to pots on the back porch.

Fresh basil is the perfect match for fresh tomatoes!

Spearmint and regular mint are also confined to containers.

Berries:

Our patch of thornless red raspberries used to only produce enough to feed the birds. This year we gave them more water, and the crop was astounding. Amazingly, we also grow blueberries successfully. Rick put them in wooden barrels on the back porch, with a slightly acid soil (which they need) and full sun.

Rick uses strawberries as a ground-cover in some flower beds, and we always get at least a handful of berries (though the birds and squirrels tend to get more than we do).

We also have two black currant bushes. The fruit is tart (almost too tart to eat) unless you let them *really* ripen. But oh, so good for you with the super-dark skins. Most people use currants to make jelly. I like it mashed as a pemmican with nuts, coconut, dates, and a dash of stevia.

Grapes:

I confess I never expected grapes would do well here. But when Rick saw the thriving home-vineyards over in Gold Country, he decided to give it a try.

Guess what: grapevines grow amazingly well, despite our short warm season! The secret is just to pick the right varieties so they're cold-tolerant. We have a separate fenced garden space devoted exclusively to grapevines, with these varieties: *Reliance; Red Flame* (red); *Himrod; Niagara; Thompson Seedless; Vanessa* (red).

We also have a beautiful grape arbor over the steps down to the garden, growing over a sturdy welded metal frame.

Clusters of grapes hang under the arbor. A trap helps keep the yellow-jackets in check.

Fruit:

Our orchard includes several types of apples: *Jonagold; Arkasas Black; Gala;* and *Red Delicious*. We also have two wonderful Peach trees, and one Pear, although the pear produces only small quantities of fruit. And our neighbors share their bounty of wonderful cherries and plums.

If you've lived here for long you know the calendar is unpredictable. We often get a late frost . . . and there goes the fruit. But we tend to get a good fruit crop about every 2-3 years and when we do, we make the most of it by freezing, drying, or canning the excess. Our dehydrator comes in especially handy for making apple chips, with all our apple trees!

Cantaloupe and watermelons also both grow here, though perhaps due to the short growing season, melons tend to be on the small side. But they're still sweet and tasty!

Flowers:

Rick is always trying something new in the flower gardens. Varieties that grow well here include: *columbine; foxglove; marigold; spider plant; day lillies; lupine; poppies; peonies; pansies;* and *violas*. Most are perennials, or come back year after year from seed without replanting. (Our pansies even cross-pollinate and pop up from seed with their own unique color patterns!)

We try to save as many seeds as we can from year to year. Snow peas; heirloom tomatoes; peppers of all kinds; and herbs like basil and cilantro all do wonderfully from saved seed. Flowers like snapdragons and bronzed daisies produce interesting color mixes and patterns in subsequent generations. Just make sure your seeds are perfectly dry before sticking them in plastic baggies. We use masking tape and a felt marker to label them with the variety and year, so we don't forget.

The one big exception for seed-saving: squashes. Plants in the squash family cross-breed so readily we found ourselves getting "acorn-zucchini" and other strange hybrids.

Catalogs:

Sitting down during those cold winter days to flip through the pages of the gorgeous full-color seed catalogs and choosing what to order for next year has become an annual "waiting for Spring" ritual. Here some of Rick's favorite seed catalogs:

- *Park Seed*
- *Rare Seeds .com*
- *Seeds 'n Such*
- *Seeds of Change*
- *Select Seeds*
- *T's Seeds*
- *Territorial Seeds*

Supplies:

And just what do you start all those seedlings in? To be sure the roots have plenty of room, look for wide, deep plastic six-paks and four-paks at a gardener's supply house. We order ours online from *JungSeed.com*. And yes, we save and recycle them from year to year until they've become too shredded by the sun.

Planting Mix:

Rick buys regular potting soil mix — bags and bags of it, stocking up during the early spring sales. He dumps one bag at a time in a sturdy plastic tub, adding water if needed to re-moisten the potting mix. Then he fills the cells of his six-paks or four-paks so they're ready for planting.

A flower garden by our rock wall.

Grass clipping piles await their turn to be returned to the soil.

Preparing the Soil & Tools, Tools, Tools

Nothing is ever wasted in Rick's garden. Grass clippings, cuttings from tender plants he's cut back — it all goes back to the soil and gets plowed under in the garden. The one exception: weeds that have already gone to seed. No need to give those "bad seeds" a head start in the garden.

Rick keeps two big, circular wire mesh "bins" for grass clippings from the lawnmower. After everything has been harvested and the ground turned under once for winter, he spreads the piles and turns the clippings under as well, so they have all winter to decompose.

In the spring each year he also adds chicken manure as a soil amendment (roughly eight large bags to a 30 x 30-foot garden plot). If his tomatoes have developed end rot the previous year, he'll add calcium or bone meal to the soil, too.

The "workhorse" of the garden is Rick's quad. This leg-saver not only takes him everywhere but hauls plants, heavy bags, weeds, branches and heavy rocks with ease. A small trailer attaches to the back with a simple ball-hitch. It's a "dump trailer" style, with a removable rear panel that makes it easy to unload.

Other must-have tools for our garden (not shown here) include a Rototiller to turn the soil in the spring, and a smaller Mantis tiller for tight quarters and hard-to-reach places.

A gas-powered chipper shreds small limbs, branches, and dead flower stalks. Those all go back into the garden, too.

The trusty quad and its dump trailer.

A rolling hand-tiller is a fast and easy way to keep the soil loose between rows in the early stages of the garden's growth, while a Hula-hoe is Rick's tool of choice for everyday weeding.

My own favorite gardening tool is a collapsible bucket for weeds and flower debris. Light, portable, and water resistant, ours arrived as a gift from Fiskar, a high-quality garden-tool maker, and has lasted more than 15 years. We love their tough, well-made clippers and loppers, too.

Chipper.

Hand-tiller.

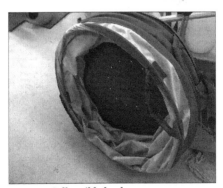
Collapsible bucket.

Gardening the High Sierra

Two tidy rows of onions.

Planting, Weeding & Irrigation

Planting:

Onions, snow peas, and other cold-hardy plants are planted directly in the garden when spring rolls around. As Rick discovered the hard way, mice amd voles are particularly fond of young, tender snow pea shoots and sprouting seeds! So he protects them while they're sprouting with lengths of fine-mesh wire screen, bent into a flattened U-shape, and the open ends get blocked off with boards. Once the

Folded wire screens protects tender snow pea seedlings from mice.

peas are up about 2-3 inches, the mice seem to lose interest, so the screens can be removed.

Tomatoes get their start in the greenhouse and are set out in neat rows after all danger of frost is gone. Rick uses sturdy round wire baskets for support. (Rick uses the tall ones — about 2-1/2 to 3 feet in height after the wire legs are inserted in the ground.) Strong baskets are a must — it's nothing for our tomato bushes to reach four to six feet tall!

A tiny bit of tending is required; one of Rick's favorite spring activities is walking the rows of the tomato patch, tucking wayward branches back into the basket for support as the plants get taller. No need to tie the tomato plants to the wire cages; the baskets alone are sufficient. And of course they get saved each fall and re-used again next year.

Rick wastes no space! Tomato rows are three feet apart; individual plants are also spaced three feet apart.

The fruit orchard, too, sees intensive planting. Rick uses the rows between trees for additional crops including beans, squashes, cucumbers, and oh yes, more tomatoes!

The main garden space gets ringed with a row of basil and dill along the edges. And cilantro seems to pop up just about everywhere on its own, thanks to previous years' crops. Both cilantro and dill have seeds that go *everywhere*! Chop it out if you insist on neat rows . . . Rick tends to let a certain amount flourish where it's planted itself.

Umbrellas of dill sprout in the main garden from seeds that "planted themselves."

Gardening the High Sierra

Weeding:

Constant attention to weeds, of course, is a necessary evil. Rick is out in his garden every morning before the day gets too hot, chopping out whatever weeds have sprouted from the night before. Amazingly, dozens of weeds put in an appearance overnight! Rick's favorite weeding tool: a Hula-hoe. The fixed blade on the end has a wiggle, letting you lop the top off the weed, no bending required.

A Hula-hoe.

Irrigation:

Rick's simple and practical solution for watering: lengths of galvanized pipe, with a hose fitting on one end; a cap on the other; and plastic sprinklers on risers set at eight-foot intervals. Perpendicular "legs" at each end of the pipe run keep the sprinklers upright. In the main garden, a length of garden hose connects one run of irrigation pipe to a second one so both water at the same time.

The upright sprinkler heads are three feet high, allowing them to water a wide area effectively from above. And of course the pipe lengths are drained, stored for the winter, and re-used, year after year.

Rick built a similar arrangement over our raspberry patch, using the metal trellis at each end to hold the galvanized pipe in place. Again, it is fed with a simple hose connection.

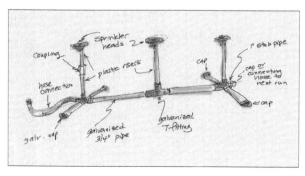

Rows of tomatoes in baskets, with irrigation line and raised sprinkler heads between the rows.

Berry patch with overhead sprinklers.

Garden Pests

It's a constant battle fighting moles, voles, rabbits, mice, chipmunks, ground squirrels and the occasional gopher. Then there are those the cute-but-hungry deer, and those not-so-cute bears. Less common but still pests: kangaroo rats and packrats. We've also got flocks of voracious magpies, bluejays, and quail (or "flying cows," Rick calls them). And then there are all the insect-pests: tomato worms, coddling moths, yellow jackets, and stink bugs. It's easy for a gardener to get discouraged, with all those armies working against you!

A certain amount of "share with the wild ones" just comes with gardening territory. But we do what we can to preserve a fair share of the bounty for us, too! Here's what's worked for Rick (and what hasn't) to keep his garden safe from as many predators as possible.

Four-Legged Pests:

To keep the deer and bears out, sturdy fencing is a must. Rick's garden has railroad ties as the posts at each corner, with five-foot horse fencing stretched all the way around. An electrified top wire will zap (but not hurt) nosy deer and bear neighbors, encouraging them to forage elsewhere.

Deer need a running start to hurdle fences this tall, so the other innovation that helps deter them is three-foot run of parallel fencing. This helps ensure they "can't get close enough to jump" the outer fence, and has worked really well to keep them out of our orchard.

A double fence (one tall, one short) helps deter deer.

Bear have great noses and are said to be able to smell ripe fruit from miles away. And as we've found out the hard way, even tightly-stapled horse fencing won't keep a really determined bear out of an orchard! We make it a point to clean up all dropped fruit quickly. And again, the electrified top wire seems to help. Remove the incentive by picking up dropped fruit and harvesting promptly.

To keep the cute cottontail bunnies and long-legged jacks out of our garden, Rick added a layer of three-foot narrow-gauge chickenwire all around the perimeter of the garden, wrapping it around the bottom of the horse fence. To make sure the squirrels can't dig underneath (and believe me, they've tried!) he dug a trench 6 to 8" deep and made sure the wire extends below the ground's surface, too.

Voles tend to be more of a problem in our lawn, while moles sometimes invade the garden, despite the protective wire fencing. So how do you know what you've got, and which one's which?

Moles are insect-eaters, with a pointy snout and big, paddle-like front feet for digging. It's rare that you'll ever see them, as they spend most of their life underground. Voles live in underbrush and create trails through your grass, especially under a coating of snow. They eat roots, seeds, and will happily feast on whatever vegetation is around in your garden.

Here's how to tell moles and voles apart by their tell-tale signs. Underground burrowers (they're looking for grubs and insects), moles leave raised mounds of dirt that look like miniature "volcanos" where they've come to the surface, and trails of raised dirt where they've tunneled below. (Sometimes you'll feel the earth give as you step on the tunnel, even though the surface doesn't appear disturbed.) Voleslike to hide in flower beds or other areas where they can hide in vegetation, and create "runs" in the edges of a lawn. You'll often see these come to light when the snow covering melts off.

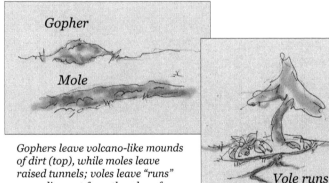

Gophers leave volcano-like mounds of dirt (top), while moles leave raised tunnels; voles leave "runs" spreading out from the edge of a planter bed or vegetation.(right).

Rick doesn't trap gophers; the best remedy is poisoned bait in the holes, though he won't use poison in the garden.

Rick must have tried 99% of the mole and vole remedies on the market, and many simply haven't been effective for him. There doesn't seem to be a good way to live-trap them, unfortunately. He's tried spring-loaded pointy jaw-traps without much success, smokers, and even an expensive gunpowder-loaded air-killing model that didn't work on our moles at all. Well-intentioned ground-thumping "sonic" deterrents have proven equally unhelpful, at least in our garden.

So, what *has* worked? For moles, Rick's had marginal success using poisoned bait, though it's terribly expensive. The best deterrent he's found for moles is a product called MoleMax which contains castor bean oil. It leaves a smell in the ground the moles don't like. If used correctly, you can slowly chase them out of your yard.

As for voles, a simple garden-variety mousetrap, placed right along their run, and/or poisoned bait, have worked best.

Squirrel damage to rock wall.

Ground squirrels also dig burrows, but their holes are larger. They are fond of burrowing into rock walls, and you may see sloughing and large piles of dirt that look like the image above.

Have-A-Hart trap catches but doesn't hurt the ground squirrels.

A top-fill bait station designed to help keep dogs and other animals from eating the poisoned bait.

To catch ground squirrels, Rick sets Have-a-Hart traps with peanuts as the lure. We don't often get chipmunks, but occasionally he'll catch a chipmunk or kangaroo rat in the Have-a-Hart trap as well. Poisoned bait is another option for keeping the ground squirrel, mouse, and chipmunk populations under control, though it's not everyone's favorite solution. If you do use poisoned bait, be sure to keep it safely away from birds, dogs, and other pets.

Bird Pests:

Birds (including those adorable quail) are totally voracious! We've found magpies and bluejays happily devouring our tomatoes, and they can do major damage to the raspberry, apple and peach crops.

Yard art that moves.

A certain amount of bird-sharing just has to go on in any garden. But Rick has found two deterrents that at least help with keeping the birds away. Wind-driven "yard art" that spins and flashes when the breeze blows seems to make birds think twice about landing nearby. And metallic bird tape that catches the sun and flashes as the wind moves is easy to attach to fencing and tomato cages, and seems to help deter winged visitors.

Metallic "bird tape" flashes as the wind catches it.

Insect Pests:

Here's Rick's best advice for controlling some of the biggest insect pests that attack our garden:

For tomato worms, he applies B.T. —short for *bacillus thuringiensis*, an organism that kills the tomato worm but won't harm humans.

Yellow jackets feast on the sugary-sweet taste of our grapes, apples, and ripe peaches, and nobody enjoys a yellow jacket sting. A simple trap with attractant bait inside helps keep these pests under control.

Coddling moths are the culprits that create bugs in your apples. We've tried bacteria-based various sprays (harmless to humans), which help reduce the number of bugs, if applied several times at just the right stage (while the tree is blooming, before fruit has set). It's a trick to get trees sprayed here effectively, though, as the time for application coincides with the windiest season. This year we also tried coddling moth traps, a sticky trap that uses a pheromone attractant. Our timing wasn't perfect but we'll probably try them again and hope for better luck.

Yelow jacket and Coddling moth traps.

The latest insect pest attacking our garden has been stink bugs. A recent non-native invader, these bugs were unknown here until just a few years ago. Remedies include diatomaceous earth, although that only works if you get it right on the bug and requires multiple applications, as they reproduce quickly. Pyrethrins are also recommended as a possible remedy.

Stink bug

One fence isn't enough. The horse fence around Rick's main garden has an extra added layer of chicken wire on the lower portion, to keep out bunnies and other critters.

We're always looking for new safe and non-toxic pest remedies, so please let us know if you've found something that works well in *your* garden!

Keeping What You Grow
Canning, Freezing, Dehydrating, & Pickling

Canning:

Late August/early September is "tomato time" in the Dustman household. There's regular and "hot" tomatoes to be canned; tomato sauce and tomato soup to put up; and "sun-dried" tomatoes to dry. Oodles of canned green beans, frozen peppers, and dried beans find their way into Mason jars and freezer bags, then onto our pantry shelves and into the deep freeze for the coming year. It's a lot of work. But there's nothing quite as satisfying as a hot bowl of something tasty from your larder when the snow's three feet deep outside on the ground!

There are actually two types of home preserving. There's the regular stovetop canning process, commonly known as the "hot bath" method. Then there's pressure-cooking, which is usually reserved for preserving products that are non-acid and have meat in them, like chili, or making fast work of cooking dried beans. Here are Rick's tips for both types of home canning.

First and foremost: Be sure you're using *real* canning jars. If it doesn't have "Mason," Kerr," or "Ball" on the jar, the glass may not be designed to withstand the intense heat and pressure of canning.

Second, don't skimp when it comes to buying lids. Bargain-basement canning lids may not always seal properly. We haven't had good luck with "re-usable" plastic canning lids, either. Choose a name-brand metal canning lid and sturdy metal rings. And it probably goes without saying, but don't try to recycle previously-used lids, either. It's not worth wasting all your hard work to have jars that won't seal.

Hot Bath: Perfect for canning tomatoes, the "hot bath" method just requires filling canning jars with produce and water, then immersing them in boiling water for an appropriate length of time to kill any bacteria. The cooking pushes out some of the air inside the jar, pulling a vacuum and sealing the lids tight.

To hot-bath tomatoes, begin by dropping your tomatoes into pot of boiling water for a few seconds until the skins begin to blister, then transfer them to cold water. Use a sharp knife to core the tomatoes and quarter the tomatoes. The skins should pull off easily. We keep the prepared tomatoes in a stainless steel or glass bowl (not aluminum) until we're ready to fill the jars.

Sterilize pint or quart jars by running them through a hot dishwasher cycle. Then fill with prepared tomatoes, adding 1/2 tsp. salt and 1 tsp. vinegar to each pint (double that for quarts); then top with water to bring the level to 1/2" to 1" below the top of the jar. We sometimes add a small slice of jalapeno in the bottom of each jar for a an extra bit of zing (what we call "hot" tomatoes).

Boil rings and lids on the stovetop for a few minutes to sterilize them as well. Screw the lids on the filled jars until just snug-tight; don't over-tighten.

Fill a large canning pot with water, and add the jars. We use a metal jar-rack inside the pot that holds the jars firmly in place and keeps the glass from directly touching the extra-high heat on the bottom. (Caution: Don't put cold jars in hot water, or hot jars in cold water or on a cold surface, or your jars might break!)

Bring the filled canning pot to boiling, and cook at a full, rolling boil, covered, for 30 minutes. Remove the jars carefully from the hot water. (Canning supply stores sell a two-handled pinching jar-gripper that's perfect for this step!)

Place the hot jars on a *wooden* or other insulating surface, *not* directly on a cold countertop, and tighten each ring. You'll start to hear a series of satisfying "pops" as the jars cool down and seal. Once the jars are cool, check the tops to be sure all of them popped down completely. (If any have failed to seal, store in refrigerator and use immediately.) Let the jars cool; then label with a marking pen.

Pressure Cooking: Pressure cooking, as we've said, is great for spaghetti sauce, chili, or other products which contain meat. It's also a quick way to cook and tenderize dried beans, and helps neutralize an enzyme in green beans to make the canned product last longer.

A pressure cooker brings the temperature of its contents up past the 212-degrees Fahrenheit at which water normally boils. There's both high pressure and high heat inside a pressure-cooker, and I was always taught to be extremely nervous around them. It's true that older models had the potential to cause serious burns and injuries. Thankfully, newer models now come with a "lock-button" safety feature that won't allow the lid to be opened until it's safe to do so. So they're much less dangerous than they used to be. Even so, of course, follow directions carefully and *never* try to hurry things along by defeating the built-in safety lock!

For green beans, wash and snap the beans; pack them gently into jars; then add a pinch of salt to each pint and fill with water to within 1" of the top of the jar.

Fill the pressure cooker with boiling water to its lowest fill mark on the inside of the pot. Put the lid on, but don't add the pressure regulator to the top of the lid yet. Bring the pot to a boil until steam begins to show; then set a timer and steam for five minutes.

Add the pressure regulator to the top and continue to cook. Once the regulator begins to bobble, cook for another 10 minutes, then turn off heat. Let the pressure inside the pot drop naturally. If any steam is still escaping, do not attempt to open! The plug-lock will eventually drop on its own.

Once the plug-lock drops, let the pot sit at least another 10 minutes to continue cooling. Then remove the pressure cooker lid, carefully lift out the jars, placing them on a wooden or insulated surface, and tighten the rings.

Freezing:

We freeze all kinds of fruit when it's in season to use later in smoothies and in baked goods. Peaches, apples, grapes, and pears, all get washed, cut up, and placed into freezer bags, or portioned into single-serving plastic storage containers.

We also freeze blueberries, strawberries, and currants from our garden. One helpful tip for berries: To keep them from clumping into a solid frozen mass, we wash and place berries individually on a plastic or metal tray, then pop the tray into the fridge for about an hour. Once the berries are little frozen marbles, we take them off the tray and put them into freezer bags.

Dehydrating/Drying:

We love our Excalibur food dehydrator (a square model, not one of the round dehydrators). It holds nine 15-inch-square trays.

We've used it to make dried tomatoes; apple chips; and dried onion slices. It's also a great way to preserve all sorts of excess fruit. Just blend together in a blender and spread the slurry on teflon dehydrator sheets, and make your own "fruit roll-ups."

Mint growing on our back porch.

We also air-dry herbs from our garden like mint, dill, and cilantro. Just rinse and lay herbs on paper towels on your kitchen counter for a day or two until thoroughly dry, then place the dried herbs in baggies or (better yet) glass jars.

Pickling:

Rick has become a major fan of making homemade pickles, since he found a recipe that recreates the flavor of dill pickles his neighbor used to make when he was a child. (Find the recipe in the Recipes section that follows.)

Although we haven't experimented with pickling beyond his dill pickle success, other friends have successfully pickled a wide variety of colorful vegetables, including carrots, onions and beets. And sauerkraut, of course, is another favorite pickling gem!

So if you're in the mood to try pickling, hunt up a great recipe online and go for it! It's another great way to preserve all your garden goodness.

Recipes

Here are some of our favorite recipes, using produce from our High Sierra garden! We hope you'll enjoy these as much as we do.

Roasted Tomato Soup

4 cups fresh tomatoes
3 cloves garlic
2 medium yellow onions
3 c. vegetable stock
1/4 c. extra-virgin olive oil
2 bay leaves
salt and pepper to taste

Preheat oven to 450 degrees. Wash and core tomatoes (no need to peel them); cut in half, and distribute among two or three glass or ceramic baking trays. Mince garlic and chop onions coarsely; add to the baking trays.

Drizzle the tomatoes and onion mixture with olive oil; season with salt and pepper.

Place in the oven and roast for 30 to 35 minutes, until juices begin to caramelize and peaks of tomatoes and onions are slightly blackened.

Carefully transfer the contents of the baking tray to a large cooking pot. Add vegetable stock and bay leaves and bring to a boil; then reduce heat and simmer about 30 minutes, to slightly thicken.

Carefully ladle about a third of the soup mixture into a blender (removing the bay leaf), and blend until smooth. Transfer the blended soup to a large cooking pot or bowl, and continue ladling and blending all of the soup has been processed.

Heat the soup through again, if you plan on serving immediately, or pour into pint canning jars and hot-bath the jars for 25 minutes to seal.

Makes approx. 7 pints of soup.

Tomato & Red Pepper Soup

20 fresh tomatoes
1 to 2 large red onions, chopped coarsely
6 - 8 mild red Anaheim peppers, cut in thin strips
flour
olive oil
tarragon
dash hot red pepper
salt

Dunk tomatoes in boiling water to remove skins, and chop slightly (or use canned tomatoes, reserving liquid). If you plan to can the soup, also get another pot of water boiling for the hot-bath.

In a large metal cooking pot, saute the onions in a generous amount of olive oil (3-4 Tb.). When onions are transparent, add Anaheim peppers and pinch of tarragon. Saute well.

Add 1 to 2 Tb. flour and stir, adding reserved tomato juice or water to make a thick roux. When the flour is cooked, add the tomatoes, a dash of hot pepper, and salt to taste.

Cook the soup for 30 to 45 minutes, until thickened. Remove half the soup and puree in a blender, then add back to your cooking pot to make a smoother soup.

Enjoy immediately, or pour into clean pint jars and hot-water bath for 25 minutes to seal; then tighten lids.

Seasoned Black Beans (Pressure-Cooker Method)

Rinse 1 pound bag of dry black beans (approx. 2 cups) in a colander, then pick over the beans to remove any small rocks or dirt.

Place the beans in a medium saucepan and cover with water. Bring to a rolling boil, then turn off heat and let sit for one hour. Drain water (this helps get rid of enzymes).

Add the beans to small pressure cooker with the following ingredients and seasonings:

> 2 pints canned tomatoes *or* 4 c. water
> 1 onion, chopped
> olive oil (2-3 Tb.)
> pinch red (hot) pepper
> cumin (1 tsp.)
> salt and pepper to taste

Close the lid on pressure cooker, and add the bobbler. Heat until the indicator begins to bobble, then cook another <u>five minutes</u> (approx. 20-25 minutes cooking time, total). Turn pressure cooker off and let cool thoroughly before opening.

Cilantro Pesto

Wash a large quantity of fresh cilantro. (We pick a heaping mound in a large cooking bowl.) Remove the largest stems and chop slightly.

Blend the fresh cilantro in a food processor with:

- 1/2 c. olive oil
- 1/4 c. lemon juice
- salt to taste
- pinch hot red pepper

Using a rubber spatula, fill plastic or rubberized ice cube trays with the cilantro mixture; freeze until solid.

When the cubes are frozen, pop them out of the ice cube trays, and store the cubes in freezer-bags in your freezer.

A wonderful pesto topping for a dish of black beans and brown rice, especially with slices of fresh tomato on top!

Panazella (Salad)

- 3 Tb. olive oil
- 1 small loaf of French bred, cubed (6 c.)
- 1 tsp. salt
- 2 large tomatoes, cubed
- 1 cucumber, sliced 1/2" thick
- 1 red bell, cut into 1" x 1" pieces
- 1 yellow bell, ditto
- 1/2 red onion, sliced thinly
- 20 large basil leaves, cut into strips
- 3 Tb. capers, drained

Assemble ingredients and prepare vegetables. Set aside.

Also prepare the vinaigrette, whisking the following ingredients together, then set aside:

3 Tb. mild vinegar of your choice
1/2 c. olive oil
1/2 tsp. Dijon mustard
1 tsp. minced garlic
1/2 tsp. salt
black pepper to taste

Heat oil in a large, deep saute pan. Add bread cubes and salt and cook over low heat, stirring frequently, until bread is browned (approx. 7-10 min.).

In a large serving bowl, mix salad ingredients together with the vinaigrette. Add bread cubes last, and toss again slightly. Serve immediately.

Zucchini Soup
(A great way to use up all those fresh zucchini!)

2 medium zucchinis
1/4 c. extra-virgin olive oil
1/4 c. chopped fresh basil
2 Tb. lemon juice (approx. 1/2 fresh lemon)
1 clove garlic
salt
pepper

Cut ends off zucchini, and quarter them. Cook for 7-8 minutes in boiling hot water, until zucchini is tender.

While the zucchini is cooking, add remaining ingredients to a blender jar. When zucchini is cooked, drain and add to the blender as well.

Blend well on high until basil is well blended and mixture is smooth. Serve immediately while hot, or refrigerate and enjoy as a cool, refreshing summer soup.

Tasty Green Beans

Wash and snap about 2 c. fresh green beans. Boil for about 8 minutes, until tender. While the beans are cooking, assemble in a small container:

    2 Tb. almond flour
    1/4 tsp. garlic powder
    1/2 tsp. salt
    1/4 tsp. black pepper

Stir dry ingredients together until well blended.

When beans are tender, drain and pour into a serving dish. Sprinkle with almond mixture and toss to coat.

Optional: drizzle top with 2 Tb. olive oil before serving.

Grandma Levoff's Kosher Dill Pickles

Wash and sterilize a gallon-sized jar to put the pickles in.

20-25 small cucumbers (3 to 4 inches long)
8 cloves garlic
2-3 large stalks of dill
8 cups of brine
(To make brine: Mix 8 cups water with 1/2 c. Kosher salt, *not* iodized salt; heat half the water to dissolve the salt, then add the rest of the water to cool the mixture down more quickly.)

Prepare cucumbers by washing, then slice off a tiny bit of the blossom end. (This helps keep pickles crisp.)

Pack the pickles tightly in the glass jar, with the first row standing upright. Add dill and garlic on top of the first layer. Continue layering by packing tightly with additional layers of pickles. (Tight packing is required so the pickles don't float to the top and spoil.)

Fill the jar with brine and place a small glass object on the top to keep pickles under the level of the brine. It's important that *nothing* protrude over the surface of the water, as this is where bacteria attacks and spoils the pickle batch.

Keep the jar of pickles on your countertop for about 7 days. A white dust will begin to appear on the pickles; this is *normal* and means the pickling process has begun. By the end of 7 days the white dust will have begun to settle to the bottom of the jar.

Using a *clean hand*, sample the pickles to see if they are ready. When crisp and tangy, transfer to a clean container and store in the refrigerator. They will keep for several months (we've seen them keep up to a year!)

Solstice Chili
(A bright, warm celebration meal to welcome the Solstice every December 21st, and help you begin to think thoughts of Spring!)

Chop/prepare:
1/2 large yellow onion
2 cloves garlic
1/2 red bell pepper

Mix seasonings in small bowl:
1 tsp. chili powder
2 tsp. cumin
1/2 tsp. coriander
1/4 tsp. cinnamon

Also prepare/measure out:
1-1/2 c. vegetable stock (measure and set aside)
(1) 14-oz. (pint) jar canned tomatoes, with juice
1 can kidney beans, drained
1 can black beans, drained

3/4 c. uncooked bulgar (measure and set aside)
1 Tb. red wine vinegar
1 Tb. chipotle adobo
1-1/2 tsp. paprika (measure and set aside; add at very end).

<u>Toppings if desired</u>:
Cheddar cheese, grated
3 Tb. cilantro, chopped

Begin a pot of rice if you plan to serve the chili over rice.

Place 1-1/2 Tb. olive oil in a large, deep stew pot. When the oil begins to ripple, add onion, garlic, and peppers. Cook about 7-8 minutes, until onion is translucent.

Add spice mix and stir 1-2 minutes, until spices are well-mixed with onions and fragrant. Add the vegetable stock, tomatoes, drained beans, dry bulgar, vinegar, and adobo.

Bring to a boil, then reduce heat and simmer about 25-30 minutes. Sauce will thicken, and the bulgar will be tender.

Stir in paprika just before serving. (I love it served over rice.) Garnish each bowl if desired with cheese and chopped cilantro.

Happy Gardening!

Made in the
USA
Lexington, KY